ALEXANDRIA
OCASIO-CORTEZ

ALEXANDRIA OCASIO-CORTEZ

••• POLITICAL HEADLINER •••

ANNA LEIGH

LERNER PUBLICATIONS ◆ MINNEAPOLIS

For Courtney

Lerner Publications Company
An imprint of Lerner Publishing Group, Inc.
241 First Avenue North
Minneapolis, MN 55401 USA

For reading levels and more information, look up this title at www.lernerbooks.com.

Image credits: Win McNamee/Getty Images, pp. 2, 6, 29; Scott Heins/Getty Images, pp. 8, 9, 19, 23; Scott Kowalchyk/CBS/Getty Images, p. 10; David L. Ryan/The Boston Globe/Getty Images, p. 13; Robert Gauthier/Los Angeles Times/Getty Images, p. 14; Brett Carlsen/Getty Images, p. 15; Emily Molli/Anadolu Agency/Getty Images, p. 17; DON EMMERT/AFP/Getty Images, pp. 18, 27; Slaven Vlasic/Getty Images, p. 21; Spencer Platt/Getty Images, p. 22; J Pat Carter/Washington Post)/Getty Images, p. 24; Tom Williams/CQ Roll Call/Getty Images, pp. 28, 30; SAUL LOEB/ AFP/Getty Images, p. 31; Alex Wong/Getty Images, pp. 32, 37; Cheriss May/NurPhoto/Getty Images, p. 33; BRENDAN SMIALOWSKI/AFP/Getty Images, p. 34; Alex Wroblewski/Getty Images, p. 35. Cover images: MANDEL NGAN/AFP/Getty Images.

Main body text set in Rotis Serif Std 55 Regular.
Typeface provided by Adobe Systems.

Library of Congress Cataloging-in-Publication Data

Names: Leigh, Anna, author.
Title: Alexandria Ocasio-Cortez : political headliner / Anna Leigh.
Description: Minneapolis : Lerner Publications, 2020. | Series: Gateway biographies | Includes bibliographical references and index. | Audience: Ages 9–14 | Audience: Grades 4–6 | Summary: "American politician Alexandria Ocasio-Cortez is the youngest woman ever to serve in the US Congress. Learn about the most fascinating details of her life and her career in the House of Representatives"—Provided by publisher.
Identifiers: LCCN 2019028046 (print) | LCCN 2019028047 (ebook) | ISBN 9781541577473 (library binding) | ISBN 9781541588875 (paperback) | ISBN 9781541583054 (ebook)
Subjects: LCSH: Ocasio-Cortez, Alexandria, 1989- —Juvenile literature. | United States. Congress. House—Biography—Juvenile literature. | Women legislators—United States— Biography—Juvenile literature. | Legislators—United States—Biography—Juvenile literature.
Classification: LCC E901.1.O27 L45 2020 (print) | LCC E901.1.O27 (ebook) | DDC 328.73/092 [B]—dc23

LC record available at https://lccn.loc.gov/2019028046
LC ebook record available at https://lccn.loc.gov/2019028047

Manufactured in the United States of America
1-46770-47761-9/17/2019

CONTENTS

Alexandria Ocasio-Cortez is sworn in during a congressional hearing in July 2019.

Twenty-eight-year-old Alexandria Ocasio-Cortez was on her way to an election watch party in the Bronx, New York, on June 26, 2018. For more than a year, she had been campaigning to become the district's Democratic nominee for Congress, and tonight she would find out if her efforts had been successful.

Many people thought it was unlikely she would win. Ocasio-Cortez was running against Joe Crowley, a Democrat who had been in Congress for twenty years. She had never held political office before, she was much younger than most people in Congress, and she didn't have a lot of politically experienced people on her campaign team. Her campaign also had less money than Crowley's. She had refused to accept large donations from businesses or political organizations, so her campaign had raised just hundreds of thousands of dollars compared to her opponent's millions.

Major news outlets had not bothered to cover Ocasio-Cortez's campaign, thinking there was no way she would beat Crowley. Crowley didn't take her campaign seriously either. When the two were supposed to debate as part of the campaign, he said he had scheduling conflicts and didn't show up.

Three weeks before the election, polls showed that Ocasio-Cortez was behind in the race. But Ocasio-Cortez didn't give up hope. She knew that polls tried to predict who was likely to vote in an election. Her campaign, however, targeted young people and minorities in her community—people who were considered unlikely to vote in an election like this one. If she could change the people who voted, she could change the outcome of the vote.

On Election Day, Ocasio-Cortez didn't check her phone or try to see what the early numbers were. Instead, she planned to join her campaign team and supporters to watch

Ocasio-Cortez celebrates with supporters at a victory party in the Bronx after upsetting incumbent Democratic representative Joseph Crowley on June 26, 2018.

Ocasio-Cortez cuts her victory cake at her primary election night party.

as the results came in. When she arrived at the watch party, she noticed a crowd of reporters running toward the building where her party was being held. Ocasio-Cortez started running too.

As she entered the party, she looked up at a TV and saw that the results were already in. She brought her hands to her mouth in shock as people crowded around her. She had won the election—and it wasn't close. She had won by four thousand votes.

A video of Ocasio-Cortez's reaction to her win went viral online. The news outlets that had ignored Ocasio-Cortez during her campaign finally took notice of her. They reported that her win was a huge upset, and they wondered how she had pulled it off. Newspapers and magazines wrote articles about her, and TV shows invited her to talk about her win and her political views. When she appeared on one late night talk show, the host admitted that he hadn't known her name a week earlier.

Ocasio-Cortez had not become a congresswoman yet—she still had to win the general election against Republican Anthony Pappas. But she was quickly becoming one of the most well-known politicians in the United States. People all over the country began to see Ocasio-Cortez as the future of politics. She was young, bold, and willing to speak up for working-class Americans.

She also received criticism from other politicians. They said that Ocasio-Cortez didn't understand politics or economics. They said that she had only won because she

Ocasio-Cortez went on *The Late Show with Stephen Colbert* two days after her landslide victory.

ran in a very Democratic district. Ocasio-Cortez brushed off the criticism. "I'm twenty-eight years old, and I was elected on this super-idealist platform," she said. "Folks may want to take that away from me, but I won. . . . I smoked this race. I didn't edge anybody out. I dominated. And I am going to own that."

Born in the Bronx

Alexandria's childhood wasn't like that of most politicians. She was born on October 13, 1989, in a neighborhood of the Bronx called Parkchester. Her father, Sergio Ocasio, had also grown up in the Bronx, and her mother, Blanca Ocasio-Cortez, was from Puerto Rico. Blanca had grown up in poverty and moved to the United States after marrying Sergio. Sergio owned an architectural company in the Bronx, and Blanca cleaned houses and worked as a secretary.

Though the family didn't have a lot of money, Sergio and Blanca thought it was important for Alexandria and her brother, Gabriel, to have a good education. They decided to move in search of better schools. With help from relatives, they saved enough money to buy a small house in Yorktown Heights, a wealthier neighborhood about forty minutes away.

Alexandria continued to spend a lot of time in Parkchester. Her father's business was still there, and they had a lot of family who lived in the area. Parkchester was a diverse neighborhood, but in Yorktown Heights,

Alexandria was one of the only students of color in her school. She said she sometimes felt like she was growing up in two different worlds—the wealthy neighborhood where she went to school and the lower-income neighborhood where her cousins lived. She was aware early on that she lived a different life from many of her cousins. Because she lived in a nicer neighborhood and went to a wealthier school, she had different opportunities available to her.

Alexandria worked hard in school. One of her favorite subjects was science. She once asked for a microscope for her birthday, and she had planned to become a doctor. However, some of her teachers didn't have faith in her. They told her she wouldn't make it into a science fair she wanted to enter, but Alexandria entered anyway. She went on to win second place in the microbiology category. As part of her prize, she had an asteroid in space named after her.

When she was seventeen, Alexandria won scholarships and took out student loans to attend Boston University, where she studied biochemistry. She was a dedicated student, and she was involved in many groups and events on campus. During her sophomore year, her father died of lung cancer. Just before he died, Ocasio-Cortez went home to visit him. She said she didn't know it was the last time she would see him, but as the visit was ending, she got the sense that it might be. She thought her father felt it too. As she was leaving, he called out to her and told her to make him proud.

During college, Ocasio-Cortez worked in the Boston office of Democratic senator Ted Kennedy.

Ocasio-Cortez was struck by the number of people who attended her father's funeral. She saw how his life had affected people her family didn't even know. She said it showed her how much influence a person could have, even without any wealth or formal power. Ocasio-Cortez went back to school a week later and worked even harder. She began studying international relations and economics instead of biochemistry. She spent a semester in Niger, West Africa, to learn about its economy. Once back in the United States, she became involved in politics, working in a US senator's office in Boston. She was one of the only Spanish-speaking people in the office, and she learned about the struggles facing undocumented immigrants. She began thinking more about the issues Americans deal with every day and knew she wanted to do something about them.

Politically Active

Ocasio-Cortez's father died just as the US economy crashed in 2008, causing millions of Americans to lose their homes and jobs. The crisis affected Ocasio-Cortez's family deeply. Because they no longer had her father's income, they were in danger of losing their home. Ocasio-Cortez's mother got jobs cleaning houses and driving a school bus, but the money she made was barely enough to afford the payments on their home.

After graduating from Boston University in 2011, Ocasio-Cortez moved back to the Bronx to help her mom. She became an educational director at the National Hispanic Institute, a nonprofit organization that helps Latino youth become leaders in their communities.

Over 860,000 US families lost their homes in 2008 after the economy's financial crisis.

Ocasio-Cortez was excited about Bernie Sanders's vision for the United States and supported his 2016 campaign.

She also got a job at a taco restaurant to earn extra money. Though her jobs didn't pay a lot, they were valuable in other ways. She met many people from different backgrounds. She worked with immigrants from around the world, and she spoke to people who struggled, as she did, to pay student loans and expensive health-care bills. Hearing people's stories, Ocasio-Cortez saw up close the effects of income inequality. She also learned to deal with people who didn't treat restaurant workers well. She learned to take criticism and ignore insults.

In 2016 Democratic senator Bernie Sanders ran against Hillary Clinton in the race to become the Democratic nominee for president of the United States. Still interested in politics, Ocasio-Cortez volunteered for his campaign. She helped find a place for his Bronx campaign headquarters, and she talked to people all over the city about Sanders's political views. She met activists, community organizers, and people fighting for better policies for women, people of color, and the environment. She felt drawn to Sanders's bold ideas about fighting income inequality and offering better health care in the United States.

Sanders did not win the Democratic nomination. After he dropped out of the race, however, people from his team started a new organization called Brand New Congress. Their plan was to find Americans who could run for Congress in the next election. They wanted to find people who shared Sanders's ideas and who could help bring about big changes in the United States. Ocasio-Cortez's brother, Gabriel, heard about Brand New Congress, and he thought she should run. He decided to submit an application for her.

Running for Office

In November 2016 Republican Donald Trump won the election to become president of the United States. Soon after, Ocasio-Cortez drove with some friends to Standing Rock, North Dakota. They were protesting an oil pipeline a company planned to build near the American Indian reservation there. Those protesting the pipeline were concerned that it would pollute drinking water for the reservation.

As Ocasio-Cortez was leaving Standing Rock, she got a phone call from one of the leaders of Brand New Congress.

American Indian war veterans march in protest of the Dakota Access Pipeline in North Dakota.

The organization was impressed by her application, and they were interested in having her run for Congress. At first, Ocasio-Cortez thought the idea was impossible—there was no way people would vote a server from the Bronx into Congress. But she kept speaking and meeting with people from Brand New Congress. She learned more about campaign strategies and political policy. In May 2017, she decided to run.

Ocasio-Cortez knew she would have to work hard to beat Crowley. Nobody knew who she was, and she didn't have the experience, money, or campaign team that he had. Ocasio-Cortez would have to run a different kind of campaign. "You can't really beat big money with more money," she said. "You have to beat them with a totally different game."

One advantage Ocasio-Cortez had was that she knew the district she was running in. She had grown up in this

Ocasio-Cortez and her team met with thousands of people in her district to spread the word about her campaign.

part of New York, and she still lived and spent most of her time there. It was one of the most diverse areas in the country—70 percent of those who lived there were people of color. The district was home to mostly working-class families. Ocasio-Cortez understood their lives and their struggles. Crowley, on the other hand, owned a home in a wealthier New York neighborhood and spent most of his time with his family in Virginia. Ocasio-Cortez argued that he was out of touch with the needs of the district.

Ocasio-Cortez saw it as an advantage that so many people thought her campaign would fail. No one thought she would even be able to get the 1,250 signatures she needed to get on the election ballot. She put together a small team of volunteers and started holding campaign events at people's homes. Her team made phone calls, posted on social media, and spoke to people in the community.

The campaign team was largely made up of unconventional volunteers. There were college graduates who worked in restaurants and actors and artists who knew how to tell interesting stories. They, like Ocasio-Cortez, had felt the effects of the financial crisis and understood the struggles that came along with low wages and high student loan debt. They believed in Ocasio-Cortez's political ideas, and they knew they had to run her campaign in a bold and revolutionary way.

Some of her friends designed campaign posters for Ocasio-Cortez. The posters featured a bold design and colors different from most political campaigns. Rather than using red, white, and blue, her campaign colors

Ocasio-Cortez's eye-catching campaign posters reflected her bold political platform.

were purple, blue, and yellow. These colors represented hope and unity. Since high school, she had gone by the nickname Sandy, but for the campaign, she used her full name. To further highlight her Puerto Rican heritage and the diversity in her district, her posters were written in both Spanish and English.

Ocasio-Cortez's team made a campaign video too. It showed Ocasio-Cortez getting ready in her apartment, riding the subway, and talking to people in New York City. In the video, she described her background, her views, and why she was the right candidate to represent the people of New York City. She said that New York needed leaders who were willing to speak for them.

The video went viral, and people around the country began to take notice of Ocasio-Cortez and her hopeful message. By the time the deadline for gathering signatures came around, she had gathered more than five thousand. She also raised about $200,000 in small donations. In one year of campaigning, Ocasio-Cortez and her team made 170,000 phone calls, knocked on 120,000 doors, and sent 120,000 text messages to spread her message and meet the people in her district.

Ocasio-Cortez also posted on social media often. Because many media outlets were not covering her campaign, she had to find other ways to connect with people. She liked being able to communicate directly with her followers to hear their concerns and get their feedback on her ideas. When she started her campaign, she had just three hundred followers on Twitter. A year later, she had sixty thousand.

During the campaign, a filmmaker followed Ocasio-Cortez and filmed her in action at events. Her story became part of a Netflix documentary called *Knock Down the House*. The film showed the campaigns of Ocasio-Cortez and three other women in the United States.

Director Rachel Lears speaks about her film *Knock Down the House* during an interview in May 2019.

Ocasio-Cortez said that filming the campaign as it unfolded helped her to reflect on things as they happened and to be open about the process. She hoped that sharing her campaign would help others see what was possible and inspire them to run for office.

The film came out in May 2019. Ocasio-Cortez said it ended up being inspiring for her too. "It's a reminder of the energy it took to get here, and what an enormous opportunity this is," she said. "It makes me feel like I have to squeeze every drop out of it."

Ocasio-Cortez's campaign showed what the future of politics could look like.

Because of her approach, Ocasio-Cortez became a symbol for many young Democrats. To them, she represented a new way of conducting politics and a new way of thinking about the country. Two weeks before the primary election, Democratic representative Ro Khanna of California became the only member of Congress to endorse, or publicly support, Ocasio-Cortez—even though he had already endorsed Crowley. "This is the type of person who deserves to have a shot to serve," he said when explaining why he had changed his mind. "She's doing it for all the right reasons."

A Popular Candidate

After Ocasio-Cortez won the primary election, her life changed dramatically. People started recognizing her on the street. She received hundreds of requests for interviews and media appearances. The media that had recently ignored her began writing new stories about her every day. They even gave her a new nickname: AOC. Some reports said she was a bold new face for the Democratic Party, while others said she was ruining the country. Republicans watched her especially closely, waiting for her to misspeak or make a mistake. Whenever she did, they immediately jumped in to criticize her, trying to prove that she didn't know what she was talking about.

Ocasio-Cortez's primary win drew the attention of Democrats and Republicans alike.

Ocasio-Cortez speaks to a crowd at a campaign rally for Democrat James Thompson in Wichita, Kansas, on July 20, 2018.

Ocasio-Cortez found the attention overwhelming. She said she missed being able to go out in public without being recognized or having people comment on what she was wearing or doing. Her district was strongly Democratic, so it was likely she would win the general election. But that didn't mean she wouldn't keep working hard and campaigning. Since she had gained such popularity, she began helping other candidates with their campaigns too. She traveled around the country speaking at campaign events for fellow Democrats.

When Ocasio-Cortez spoke, she talked about changing policies to protect the environment and fix the criminal justice system. She wanted to get rid of US Immigration and Customs Enforcement, or ICE, an agency that detains and deports those who have broken immigration laws. She spoke about granting all Americans health care, free tuition for public colleges, and access to good jobs that paid at least fifteen dollars an hour. Ocasio-Cortez said that these ideas were about giving all Americans the opportunity to live full and dignified lives. She thought too many Americans were working long hours at multiple jobs without being able to support their families. This, she said, was unacceptable.

Democratic Socialism

Ocasio-Cortez describes her political views as democratic socialism. Socialism is a political and economic idea that seeks to distribute wealth more evenly among the people of a country. Many in the United States associate this term with countries such as Venezuela or Cuba, where Socialist governments have gained too much power over their people. These extreme cases have led to economic issues and a lack of freedom for the people of these countries.

Others, however, associate socialism with countries like Canada or Norway, where government policies have led to better access to education and health care. This is the kind of socialism Ocasio-Cortez has in mind. Her views, she says, are pretty simple: "In a modern, moral, and wealthy society, no person in America should be too poor to live."

After giving her speeches, Ocasio-Cortez always made sure to speak directly to the people who attended. She listened carefully and took notes about their concerns. These conversations were important to her. "People tell you things," she said. "And they tell you what they believe. And they tell you what they want for themselves, for you, they tell you their stories."

Moving to Washington

Ocasio-Cortez won the general election on November 6, 2018, with more than 75 percent of the vote. Shortly after she began giving a fifteen-minute victory speech to her supporters, those in the room were disappointed to learn that another Democratic candidate had lost. Ocasio-Cortez kept her positive outlook. She reminded the crowd that individual elections don't matter as much as bringing about long-term, large-scale changes. It can take the government years to change laws and policies, so it's important to think five or ten years into the future, to the way the world will be then. Even if a candidate loses, there is still value in each campaign and the ideas they spread. Of her own race, she said, "If [the district] can be more educated, more organized, more invested than we were a year ago, then this campaign will have been one hundred percent worth it."

Following her win, other politicians such as Hillary Clinton, Bernie Sanders, and 2020 presidential

Ocasio-Cortez speaks to her supporters during her election night party.

candidate Kamala Harris reached out to Ocasio-Cortez to congratulate her and give her advice. Other Democrats in Congress reached out too. They said that they were excited to start working with her. They also warned her that it would be difficult work. They cautioned that some would pressure her to do things a certain way in Washington, DC.

Ocasio-Cortez knew she was inexperienced, and she knew she had some different ideas about politics than many in the nation's capital. There would be pressure for her to fall in line with other politicians and do things the same way as everyone else. But she didn't want to give in. She promised her supporters that she would try to bring real change to politics.

Soon after the election, Ocasio-Cortez moved to

Washington, DC, to begin an orientation program for new members of Congress. She called the orientation "Congress Camp." There, she met other members of Congress and began to learn about her new job and the government. She also had to start setting up her new office and find a new apartment.

Though Ocasio-Cortez had become well known during her campaign, the transition to life in Washington wasn't easy. When she arrived at orientation, she was mistaken for being the wife of a representative rather than a member of Congress herself. She also continued to receive criticism from other politicians. They thought she was more concerned about gaining popularity and followers on social media than about working.

Ocasio-Cortez arrives in Washington, DC, for "Congress Camp" in November 2018.

Ocasio-Cortez answers questions from the press during her orientation in Washington, DC.

Ocasio-Cortez was posting on social media, but it wasn't because she wanted more followers. Rather, she thought it was important to show people what the government was really like. She posted pictures and videos of her life—she showed herself doing laundry and eating ice cream after a long day. She answered questions about politics while cooking in her apartment, and she posted during meetings and while she was working. She thought that by being open about all the parts of her life and work, she could help end the idea that political jobs are open only to certain kinds of people. "It's so important for our community to see itself represented in leadership," she said. "And what we've shown is that you don't need access to money, to special social circles, to privilege in order to run for office."

Ocasio-Cortez picks a number to determine when she will choose congressional office space during orientation.

Ocasio-Cortez thought often of the first time she had visited the nation's capital. She went with her father when she was five. While they were there, her father told her, "You know, this is *our* government. All of this belongs to us." When she joined Congress, Ocasio-Cortez wanted to make sure that was true.

Swearing In

On January 3, 2019, Ocasio-Cortez was officially sworn in as the youngest congresswoman in US history. Later, she posted a photo of herself standing with her family and Speaker of the House Nancy Pelosi. She wrote a long caption thanking her supporters and her team. She went on to write about the hardships her family had experienced, saying that at times it had felt like there was no hope. However, she wrote, "Darkness taught me transformation cannot solely be an individual pursuit but also a community trust. We must lean on others to strive on our own."

Ocasio-Cortez took that message to heart as she began her work in Congress. Some members of Congress were still criticizing her, saying she needed to move slowly and not ask for so many changes at once. They said she needed to wait her turn and gain more experience and understanding of government processes. They wanted her to build relationships with other members of Congress so that they could work together.

Ocasio-Cortez (*center*) was determined to bring about positive change for the people in her district.

Speaking through Fashion

For her swearing-in ceremony, Ocasio-Cortez wore a bright white suit, red lipstick, and gold hoop earrings. She later explained her choice of clothing and accessories. The white suit was in honor of suffragettes—the women who first fought for women to have equal rights in the United States. They often wore white or other light colors to contrast with the dark suits men wore. White also symbolized hope and possibility. Since then, many women politicians have worn white to show their connection to suffragettes. During the 2019 State of the Union Address, all the Democratic women in Congress wore white.

Ocasio-Cortez (*center front*) and Democratic congresswomen wear white during the 2019 State of the Union Address.

Ocasio-Cortez's lipstick and earrings had a different meaning. They were for the Bronx. Growing up where she did, Ocasio-Cortez said, she and other girls were told that if they wore hoops outside the Bronx, they wouldn't be taken seriously. She also explained that Sonia Sotomayor, a Supreme Court justice from the Bronx, was told she wouldn't be taken seriously if she wore red nail polish. Sotomayor wore her red nail polish anyway. Ocasio-Cortez wore her bright lipstick and earrings to protest the idea that women in politics should look and dress a certain way.

Representative Ocasio-Cortez listens as Michael Cohen, former lawyer for Donald Trump, testifies before the House Committee on Oversight and Reform on February 27, 2019.

Many in the United States were concerned that the Democratic Party had become divided. They thought some members who were more cautious and traditional in their approach to politics might conflict with members like Ocasio-Cortez. Pelosi herself said it was important for the party to be unified and to stick to policies that all the members could support.

Ocasio-Cortez said that the differences within the Democratic Party were more about age than political ideas. Before 2019, the average age of members of the House of Representatives was fifty-eight years old. The experiences of Ocasio-Cortez and other young people in the United States had been vastly different from many in Congress. While older members had experienced a time of economic prosperity in the 1980s and 1990s, Ocasio-Cortez and others her age became adults at a time when it was difficult to pay for college, find good jobs, or afford homes. These different experiences had a large impact on the way different representatives viewed the country and its needs.

Despite having different experiences and ideas than many of her colleagues have, Ocasio-Cortez wanted to work with them. She said her priority at the beginning of her time in Congress was to listen, learn, and build relationships. She sat quietly in most meetings, taking notes and listening to other members speak.

She also met other members of Congress. Within her first few days, she had become friends with other new

Ocasio-Cortez (*right*) often works with congresswomen (*from left*) Rashida Tlaib, Ayanna Pressley, and Ilhan Omar. These politicians have become known as the Squad, and they are known for making sometimes-controversial comments.

representatives such as Rashida Tlaib, Ilhan Omar, and Ayanna Pressley. Soon she teamed up with more experienced politicians too. She worked with Massachusetts senator and presidential candidate Elizabeth Warren to release a

Ocasio-Cortez reached across the political aisle to address lobbying concerns with Republican Ted Cruz.

video and write a letter about income inequality and the actions of large businesses in the United States. She also teamed up with Republican senator Ted Cruz of Texas. They agreed to work together on a bill that would keep members of Congress from becoming paid lobbyists later in life. A lobbyist is someone who tries to convince the government to make changes that will benefit certain groups or companies. Cruz and Ocasio-Cortez said that when politicians become lobbyists, it can lead to corruption and misuses of power and government resources.

Ocasio-Cortez took her work very seriously. She spent four days a week working in Washington, and then she would go back to New York for the next three days. She said that the time she spent at home was incredibly important. She made sure to spend time with her friends and to reconnect with the people of her district. Being back in New York helped to remind her what she was working toward and who she was working for.

Green New Deal

One of Ocasio-Cortez's major concerns in her first months in Congress was climate change and the environment. Soon after arriving in Washington, she sat with some climate change activists who were protesting outside Pelosi's office. Ocasio-Cortez was nervous, and she knew she would receive some criticism for her actions. She also knew that it wasn't wrong to listen to the activists. She was curious to hear their perspectives, and she knew that activism often leads to good changes. She soon called for Pelosi to create a special climate change committee in Congress. Forty other members of Congress agreed that the committee was a good idea, and Pelosi formed the committee.

In February Ocasio-Cortez took her ideas about climate change a step further when she helped release a resolution called the Green New Deal. She had been looking at the problems facing her district in New York and the ideas that she had highlighted in her campaign, such as fair wages and access to education and health care. She realized that these were not separate issues. She didn't have to choose just one to address. Instead, the government could address all of them in similar ways. She thought that climate change was the biggest crisis facing the United States. If the country took ambitious action to fight climate change, it could solve many social and economic issues at the same time.

The Green New Deal called for Congress to come together and commit to working toward legislation that would protect the planet. The deal called for the country

Ocasio-Cortez speaks during a press conference unveiling the Green New Deal.

to commit to using only renewable energy sources within the next twelve years. As part of the plan, the United States would grant health care to all US citizens and invest in providing better wages to working Americans. The plan would also create higher tax rates for the wealthiest people in the country. This was all part of Ocasio-Cortez's vision to build a stronger future for the country and for the planet.

The media and other members of Congress immediately began criticizing the Green New Deal. They said that the deal was unrealistic, that it called for too many changes too quickly, and that there was no way to pay for these changes. They also spread the idea that Ocasio-Cortez wanted to stop people from traveling in airplanes or eating beef, even though these things were not mentioned in the resolution.

Ocasio-Cortez acknowledged that there might be other ways to reach the goal of protecting the planet. But she said the most important thing was to start a conversation. She wanted to get people thinking about the kinds of things that need to happen for the United States to successfully address society's biggest issues. "We can't compromise on saving our planet," she said. "We can't compromise on saving kids. We have to do these things."

The Future of AOC

Ocasio-Cortez's political career is just beginning, and she is already one of the best-known and most talked-about politicians in the country. People stop by her office in Washington, DC, to leave notes and encouragement, and when tourists see her, they ask her to stop and take pictures with them. Ocasio-Cortez remains committed to her ideas and her unique approach to politics. She continues to explain her views on social media and push back against those who criticize her. She released a video and appeared on TV to talk about the Green New Deal. She started a garden in Washington, DC, to help educate people about agriculture and the environment. She even spent a day working at a restaurant to advocate for better wages.

Community Garden

In April, Ocasio-Cortez announced on Twitter that she was planning to start a garden in Washington, DC, and she asked for advice about what to plant. She quickly got more than eight thousand responses. Soon she had a small garden filled with spinach, collard greens, and Swiss chard. She was excited to be able to grow her own food and do something that was good for the environment. Her garden was good for another reason too—it allowed Ocasio-Cortez to take some time out of her busy schedule to do something relaxing. While sharing pictures and videos of the garden on social media, Ocasio-Cortez was advocating for the environment as well as for both physical and mental health.

Many people wonder what Ocasio-Cortez will do next. She is often asked if she plans to spend her life working in government. Some have even thought ahead to 2028, when she'll be thirty-five years old—old enough to run for president of the United States. Ocasio-Cortez says she doesn't know exactly what the future holds, but she has always felt that it is her duty to serve people. Whether she's in Congress for just two years or much longer, she wants to think about where and how she can do the most good and serve the people of her community. "As long as I'm effective," she said, "I'll be here."

IMPORTANT DATES

October 13, 1989	Alexandria Ocasio-Cortez is born in the Bronx, New York.
September 2008	Her father, Sergio Ocasio, dies.
May 2011	Ocasio-Cortez graduates from Boston University.
November 2016	Donald Trump wins the election to become president of the United States.
December 2016	Ocasio-Cortez travels to North Dakota to protest the Dakota Access Pipeline.
	Brand New Congress calls and asks her to run for Congress.
May 2017	Ocasio-Cortez decides to run for Congress.
February 2018	She quits her job to focus on her campaign.
June 26, 2018	She wins her primary election.

November 6, 2018	She wins the general election.
January 3, 2019	She is sworn in as the youngest female member of the US Congress.
February 2019	Ocasio-Cortez and other members of Congress release the Green New Deal.
April 2019	She is listed as one of the year's one hundred most influential people by *Time* magazine.
May 2019	The documentary *Knock Down the House* is released on Netflix.

SOURCE NOTES

11 David Remnick, "Alexandria Ocasio-Cortez's Historic Win and the Future of the Democratic Party," *New Yorker*, July 16, 2018, https://www.newyorker.com/magazine/2018/07/23/alexandria -ocasio-cortezs-historic-win-and-the-future-of-the-democratic -party.

17 Aída Chávez and Ryan Grim, "A Primary against the Machine: A Bronx Activist Looks to Dethrone Joseph Crowley, the King of Queens," Intercept, May 22, 2018, https://theintercept.com /2018/05/22/joseph-crowley-alexandra-ocasio-cortez-new-york -primary/.

21 Melena Ryzick, "How Alexandria Ocasio-Cortez's Triumph, 'Ugly Crying' and All, Was Captured," *New York Times*, May 3, 2019, https://www.nytimes.com/2019/05/03/movies/knock-down-the -house-netflix.html.

22 Eliza Relman, "The Truth about Alexandria Ocasio-Cortez: The Inside Story of How, in Just One Year, Sandy the Bartender Became a Lawmaker Who Triggers Both Parties," Insider, January 6, 2019, https://www.insider.com/alexandria-ocasio -cortez-biography-2019-1.

25 "Alexandria Ocasio Cortez: Trump Isn't Ready for a Girl from the Bronx," YouTube video, 5:56, posted by *The Late Show with Stephen Colbert*, June 29, 2018, https://www.youtube.com /watch?v=Y_1G4_oPt_o.

26 Azi Paybarah, "Alexandria Ocasio-Cortez Will Push Washington. Will Washington Push Back?," *New York Times*, November 7, 2018, https://www.nytimes.com/2018/11/07/nyregion/ocasio -cortez-congress-washington.html.

26 David Weigel, "Alexandria Ocasio-Cortez: The Democrat Who Challenged Her Party's Establishment—And Won," *Washington Post*, June 27, 2018, https://www.washingtonpost.com/news /powerpost/wp/2018/06/27/alexandria-ocasio-cortez-the-democrat -who-challenged-her-partys-establishment-and-won/?utm_term =.54f4540deba0.

28 Maya Salam, "Sisterhood in the Halls of Congress, and You're Invited," *New York Times,* December 14, 2018, https:// www.nytimes.com/2018/12/14/us/politics/alexandria-ocasio -cortez-aoc-women-congress.html.

29 Andrea González-Ramírez, "Meet the Bronx-Born Puerto Rican Challenging One of the Most Powerful House Democrats," Refinery29, June 27, 2018, https://www.refinery29.com /en-us/2018/06/201503/alexandria-ocasio-cortez-new-york -congress-14th-district.

30 Remnick, "Alexandria Ocasio-Cortez's Historic Win."

31 Katherine J Igoe, "Who Is Blanca Ocasio-Cortez, Alexandria Ocasio-Cortez's Mom?," *Marie Claire*, January 31, 2019, https:// www.marieclaire.com/politics/a26099099/who-is-alexandria -ocasio-cortez-mom-blanca/.

38 Charlotte Alter, "'Change Is Closer Than We Think.' Inside Alexandria Ocasio-Cortez's Unlikely Rise," *Time*, March 21, 2019, http://time.com/longform/alexandria-ocasio-cortez-profile/.

39 Alex Morris, "Alexandria Ocasio-Cortez Wants the Country to Think Big," *Rolling Stone*, February 27, 2019, https:// www.rollingstone.com/politics/politics-features/alexandria -ocasio-cortez-congress-interview-797214/.

SELECTED BIBLIOGRAPHY

Aleksander, Irina. "How Alexandria Ocasio-Cortez and Other Progressives Are Defining the Midterms." *Vogue*, October 15, 2018. https://www.vogue.com/article/alexandria-ocasio-cortez-interview-vogue-november-2018-issue.

Alter, Charlotte. "'Change Is Closer Than We Think.' Inside Alexandria Ocasio-Cortez's Unlikely Rise." *Time*, March 21, 2019. http://time.com/longform/alexandria-ocasio-cortez-profile/.

Chávez, Aida, and Ryan Grim. "A Primary against the Machine: A Bronx Activist Looks to Dethrone Joseph Crowley, the King of Queens." Intercept, May 22, 2018. https://theintercept.com/2018/05/22/joseph-crowley-alexandra-ocasio-cortez-new-york-primary/.

Cooper, Anderson. "Alexandria Ocasio-Cortez: The Rookie Congresswoman Challenging the Democratic Establishment." *60 Minutes*, January 6, 2019. https://www.cbsnews.com/news/alexandria-ocasio-cortez-the-rookie-congresswoman-challenging-the-democratic-establishment-60-minutes-interview-full-transcript-2019-01-06/.

Golden, Hannah. "28-Year-Old Alexandria Ocasio-Cortez Is Pushing for Millennials' Future through Politics." Elite Daily, June 12, 2018. https://www.elitedaily.com/p/28-year-old-alexandria-ocasio-cortez-is-pushing-for-millennials-future-through-politics-9346653.

González-Ramírez, Andrea. "Meet the Bronx-Born Puerto Rican Challenging One of the Most Powerful House Democrats." Refinery29, June 27, 2018. https://www.refinery29.com/en-us/2018/06/201503/alexandria-ocasio-cortez-new-york-congress-14th-district.

Morris, Alex. "Alexandria Ocasio-Cortez Wants the Country to Think Big." *Rolling Stone*, February 27, 2019. https://www.rollingstone .com/politics/politics-features/alexandria-ocasio-cortez-congress -interview-797214/.

Paybarah, Azi. "Alexandria Ocasio-Cortez Will Push Washington. Will Washington Push Back?" *New York Times*, November 7, 2018. https://www.nytimes.com/2018/11/07/nyregion/ocasio-cortez -congress-washington.html.

Relman, Eliza. "The Truth about Alexandria Ocasio-Cortez: The Inside Story of How, in Just One Year, Sandy the Bartender Became a Lawmaker Who Triggers Both Parties." Insider, January 6, 2019. https://www.insider.com/alexandria-ocasio-cortez-biography-2019-1.

Remnick, David. "Alexandria Ocasio-Cortez's Historic Win and the Future of the Democratic Party." *New Yorker*, July 16, 2018. https://www. newyorker.com/magazine/2018/07/23/alexandria-ocasio -cortezs-historic-win-and-the-future-of-the-democratic-party.

Weigel, David. "Alexandria Ocasio-Cortez: The Democrat Who Challenged Her Party's Establishment—And Won." *Washington Post*, June 27, 2018. https://www.washingtonpost.com/news/powerpost/wp/2018/06/27 /alexandria-ocasio-cortez-the-democrat-who-challenged-her-partys -establishment-and-won/?utm_term=.54f4540deba0.

FURTHER READING

BOOKS

Braun, Eric. *Taking Action for Civil and Political Rights*. Minneapolis: Lerner Publications, 2017. Read about some other ordinary people who stood up to make a difference in their communities.

Howell, Janet, and Theresa Howell. *Leading the Way: Women in Power*. Somerville, MA: Candlewick, 2019. Learn about more inspiring women in politics, including the first woman elected to Congress and the first woman to sit on the US Supreme Court.

Leigh, Anna. *Nancy Pelosi: Political Powerhouse*. Minneapolis: Lerner Publications, 2020. Find out more about Speaker of the House Nancy Pelosi and her long career in government.

Mattern, Joanne. *Rising Sea Levels*. New York: Cavendish Square, 2019. Read more about climate change, its causes, and its effects to better understand why Ocasio-Cortez thinks the Green New Deal is so important.

WEBSITES

Congresswoman Alexandria Ocasio-Cortez
    https://ocasio-cortez.house.gov/
    Visit Ocasio-Cortez's government website to learn about her work in Congress and the policies she is fighting for.

"A Message from the Future with Alexandria Ocasio-Cortez"
    https://theintercept.com/2019/04/17/green-new-deal-short-film-alexandria-ocasio-cortez/
    Watch this video to learn more about the Green New Deal and Ocasio-Cortez's dream for the future.

United States House of Representatives
    https://www.house.gov/
    Find out more about the House of Representatives, current members of Congress, and the work they are doing to bring about change in the United States.

INDEX